SUPER
SOCIAL STUDIES
INFOGRAPHICS

US GOVERNMENT
THROUGH
INFOGRAPHICS

Nadia Higgins

graphics by
Alex Sciuto

Lerner Publications Company
Minneapolis

Copyright © 2015 by Lerner Publishing Group, Inc.

Lerner Publications Company
A division of Lerner Publishing Group, Inc.
241 First Avenue North
Minneapolis, MN 55401 USA

For reading levels and more information, look up this title at www.lernerbooks.com.

Main text set in Univers LT Std 12/15.
Typeface provided by Adobe Systems.

Library of Congress Cataloging-in-Publication Data

Higgins, Nadia.
    US government through infographics / by Nadia Higgins ;
illustrations by Alex Sciuto.
        pages   cm. — (Super social studies infographics)
    Includes index.
    ISBN 978–1–4677–3463–9 (lib. bdg. : alk. paper)
    ISBN 978–1–4677–4748–6 (eBook)
    1. United States—Politics and government—Juvenile
literature. I. Sciuto, Alex illustrator. II. Title.
JK40.H54 2015
320.473—dc23   2013041241

Manufactured in the United States of America
1 – PC – 7/15/14

CONTENTS

Introduction

GOVERNMENT OR BUST!

Do you have what it takes to be an expert on government? To find out, take this test:

1. Do you get a kick out of reading political bumper stickers?

2. Do you daydream about running for student council?

3. Have you ever worn an "I Voted" sticker, just for fun?

4. Do you like to think about freedom, power, and equality—and how they work?

Did you answer yes to any of those questions?

CONGRATULATIONS!

You could have a future as a political scientist. These social scientists study how government works. Many focus on just the US government. They study different parts, such as political parties or elections. They ask big questions too. What makes government successful? How can it be more fair? For answers, they look at how government is organized, how laws are made, and more.

This work often involves big numbers and LOTS of data! So political scientists use maps, charts, and other infographics to help keep their info clear and organized. Care to join them? Let's get started!

A BASIC HUMAN NEED

The first governments developed about 5,000 years ago. Early civilizations in Mesopotamia (present-day Iraq) needed to keep order in their societies and protect against enemies. These days, governments still do that—and a whole lot more.

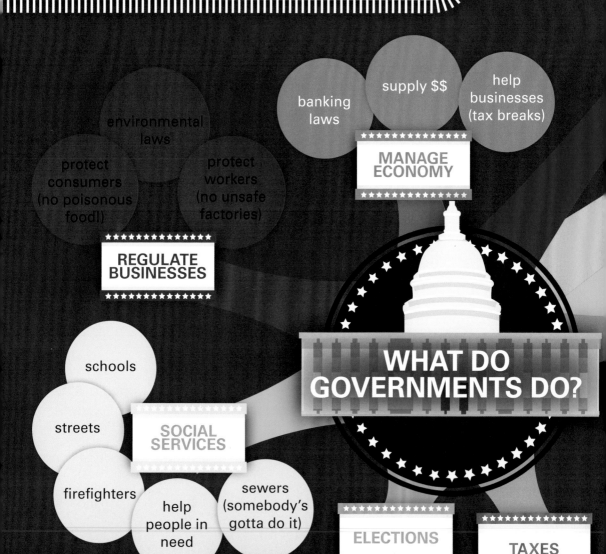

banking laws

supply $$

help businesses (tax breaks)

★★★★★★★★★★★★★★
MANAGE ECONOMY
★★★★★★★★★★★★★★

environmental laws

protect consumers (no poisonous food!)

protect workers (no unsafe factories)

★★★★★★★★★★★★★★
REGULATE BUSINESSES
★★★★★★★★★★★★★★

schools

streets

★★★★★★★★★★★★
SOCIAL SERVICES
★★★★★★★★★★★★

firefighters

help people in need

sewers (somebody's gotta do it)

WHAT DO GOVERNMENTS DO?

★★★★★★★★★★★★★★
ELECTIONS
★★★★★★★★★★★★★★

★★★★★★★★★★★★★★
TAXES

RANDOM COOL STUFF

fund the arts

parades and ceremonies

scientific and medical research (cure for cancer?)

explore space (Mars rover!)

national parks (Yellowstone all the way!)

MAKE LAWS

crime

public safety (seat belts)

marriage/ divorce

FOREIGN AFFAIRS

trade

peace talks

embassies

diplomats

immigrants/ border control

United Nations

ENFORCE LAWS

police

courts

prisons

DEFENSE

wars

train soldiers

intelligence (a.k.a. spies)

GOVERNMENT CHECK UP

Is your government in good shape? Check this list of signs of good health:

Legitimacy
Citizens believe their government has the basic right to make laws.

Freedom
Individual rights, such as free speech, are protected.

Rule of Law
Everybody follows the same laws, even those in charge.

Equality
All citizens enjoy the same basic rights and opportunities.

Transparency
The government does not operate in secret.

Sovereignty
The government operates free of outside powers.

GOVERNMENT ACROSS THE GLOBE

There are so many ways to think about a government. Who's in charge? How is it organized? Is there a constitution? But the most important question has to do with citizens. How much say do they have? Countries around the globe have been steadily moving toward democracy. Still, about 37 percent of people worldwide have no part in how government controls their lives.

UNITED KINGDOM
PARLIAMENTARY DEMOCRACY

Voters elect members of Parliament, the legislating body. Parliament picks the prime minister, who heads the government.

UNITED STATES
DEMOCRATIC REPUBLIC

Voters elect the president through the electoral college, a group that casts votes for the president on the people's behalf.

CHINA
COMMUNISM
The government owns most of the country's property, which it claims to share with all citizens. The Communist Party has been known to squash competing political parties.

IRAN
THEOCRACY
Religious leaders are in charge.

NORTH KOREA
DICTATORSHIP
A dictator or a small group of people rule harshly over citizens. Dictators make laws on a whim. They may use torture or spying to control those who resist them.

SAUDI ARABIA
TRADITIONAL MONARCHY
Rulers are born into power, which they say was given by God.

MAP KEY

 Authoritarian
Citizens live at the mercy of their rulers. Many of these countries have democracy "on paper." For example, elections are held, but no real choice is offered.

 Democratic
Citizens elect their leaders. They enjoy personal freedoms, such as the right to free speech and religion.

 **Partly Democratic**
Democratic systems are weakened by bad laws, corruption, poverty, and more. Personal freedoms are iffy.

DEMOCRACY THROUGH THE AGES

Democracy may go back as far as 10,000 years. For early civilizations, voting was a natural way to get things done. As society became more complicated, so did democracy. Two key features emerged: 1) Representation. Voters elected representatives to make laws on their behalf. 2) Universal suffrage. Voting became open to all adults. These "simple" ideas took thousands of years to develop.

Early Democracy

Around 550 BCE

Democracy develops in the city-state of Athens, in ancient Greece. Thousands of citizens gather to vote directly on laws. Women and slaves can't vote.

Around 1400

A new spirit of individual thinking spreads throughout Europe.

1689

Parliament signs the English Bill of Rights. This document greatly expands Parliament's power.

Late 1600s

English philosopher John Locke says power belongs in the hands of the people.

Revolution

1776

The Founding Fathers sign the Declaration of Independence. It asserts that government must protect individual rights.

1787

The US Constitution sets up the framework of modern democracy.

Spread of Democracy

Around 800

In Europe, feudalism is the system of the day. Most people are peasants who work like slaves for nobles. Still, laws abound. A court system develops.

Around 75 BCE

Roman statesman Cicero says humans have natural rights.

Around 1100

In Italian city-states, citizens choose representatives. Very few ordinary people get to vote, though.

Middle Ages

New Expectations

1295

King Edward I accepts an elected Parliament in England. (But only wealthy men can vote for it.)

1215

English nobles force King John to sign the Magna Carta, limiting his power. For the first time, written law has more power than the king.

1893

New Zealand is first to extend voting rights to women—27 years before the United States.

1960s

The civil rights movement expands the vote of African Americans.

Late 1800s

Most European nations have constitutions.

1950s

After gaining independence from England, India becomes the world's largest democracy.

1990s

Democracy spreads throughout eastern Europe and Latin America.

2010s

The struggle for democracy spreads to the Middle East.

CONSTITUTION, CLARIFIED

Drafted in 1787, the US Constitution lays out the basic framework of our nation's government. It clarifies the roles of states, making sure that a strong national government is still in charge. It also protects individual rights. This amazing document has lasted longer than any other written constitution in the world.

THE CONSTITUTION HAS THREE MAIN PARTS: THE PREAMBLE , THE ARTICLES , AND THE AMENDMENTS .

The Constitution was written on four large pages of treated animal skin (likely calf or sheep). It takes about half an hour to read.

The PREAMBLE

The Preamble is a short introduction. It lays out the writers' goals, including lasting peace and a fair justice system.

We the People of the United States, in Order to form a more perfect Union, establish Justice, insure domestic Tranquility, provide for the common defence, promote the general Welfare, and secure the Blessings of Liberty to ourselves and our Posterity, do ordain and establish this Constitution for the United States of America.

That fancy script says,

Article 1

The ARTICLES

The seven articles set up the basic rules of government. They outline rules for Congress, the president and the vice president, and the Supreme Court. The articles make rules for how states can get along and how to amend, or change, the Constitution.

AMENDMENTS 1-10

THE BILL OF RIGHTS
Some states refused to approve the Constitution unless it protected individual rights. That led to the first 10 amendments, known as the Bill of Rights. It was adopted in 1791.

The AMENDMENTS

An amendment is a change to the Constitution after it was signed on September 17, 1787.

No. 27
1992 If Congress votes to give itself pay raises, they won't take effect until after the next election.

No. 22
1951 A president may be elected to office only twice.

AMENDMENTS 11–27

1800 ● ● — 11 12

1900 — 13 14 15   16 17 18 19 20 21   22 23 24 25 26   **2000** — 27

No. 13
1865 Slavery is illegal.

No. 19
1920 Women have the right to vote.

No. 24
1964 The government can't use taxes as a way to keep people from voting.

BRANCHES IN BALANCE

The creators of the US Constitution were fed up with power-hungry rulers. So they set up a system of checks and balances. Three branches of government share power. Each has ways of keeping the others in line.

Congress can fire a president (though this hasn't happened yet).

EXECUTIVE BRANCH

The president heads this branch. The president is in charge of the military and foreign affairs. He or she also leads national policy and signs bills into laws.

HELP WANTED

Thinking about running for office someday? Read this first.

	REPRESENTATIVE	SENATOR	PRESIDENT
Age	at least 25	at least 30	at least 35
Citizenship	US citizen for at least 7 years	US citizen for at least 9 years	Born in the United States
Location	Live in the state you represent	Live in the state you represent	Lived on US soil for at least 14 years
Term	2 years no term limit	6 years no term limit	4 years two-term limit
Salary	$174,000	$174,000	$400,000

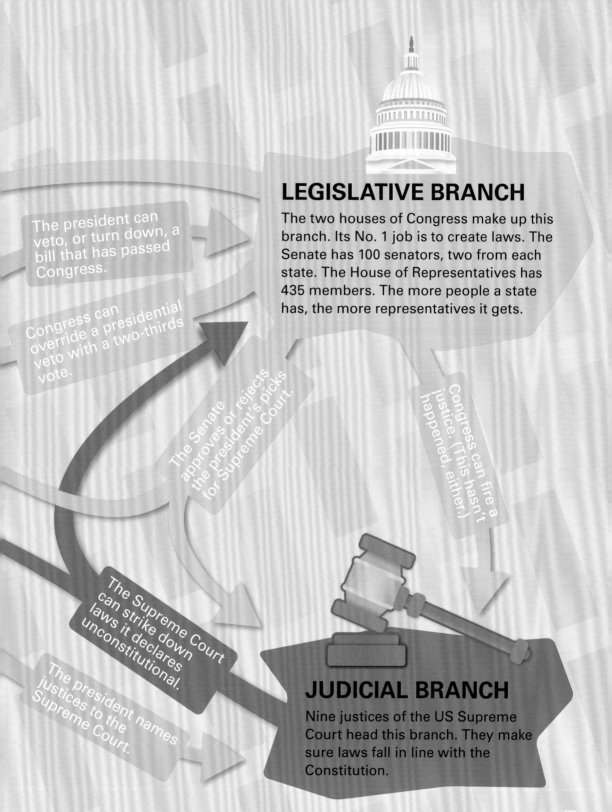

LEGISLATIVE BRANCH

The two houses of Congress make up this branch. Its No. 1 job is to create laws. The Senate has 100 senators, two from each state. The House of Representatives has 435 members. The more people a state has, the more representatives it gets.

The president can veto, or turn down, a bill that has passed Congress.

Congress can override a presidential veto with a two-thirds vote.

The Senate approves or rejects the president's picks for Supreme Court.

Congress can fire a justice. (This hasn't happened, either.)

The Supreme Court can strike down laws it declares unconstitutional.

The president names justices to the Supreme Court.

JUDICIAL BRANCH

Nine justices of the US Supreme Court head this branch. They make sure laws fall in line with the Constitution.

THREE LEVELS

The United States operates on the idea of federalism. The national government is in charge overall. But some jobs are saved for the states. In turn, states oversee local governments. Each level has its own special role.

HOT TOPICS

How might the three levels of government handle some key issues of the day?

Health Care

Federal
Passes a law saying citizens must have health insurance

State
Figures out how new insurance program will work in state

Local
Sets up a citywide bike rental system, so people get more exercise

Environment

Federal
Signs a treaty with other nations to limit pollution

State
Fines businesses that pollute too much

Local
Runs city buses that use clean energy

Business

Federal
Grants loans to business owners

State
Offers tax breaks to new businesses

Local
Provides businesses with top-notch roads, sewers, and other services

Federal Government

Role
The boss. It sets broad laws that states follow. Foreign policy happens here.

Specific Jobs
Running the military, managing Social Security, coining money

Who's in Charge
President, Congress, US Supreme Court

State Government

Role
It puts federal laws into practice. It runs the show in areas where the feds haven't spoken up.

Who's in charge
Governor, state legislature, state supreme court

Takes the Lead
On schools, elections, criminal law

Local Government

Role
Cities, counties, and towns report to states. They run the day-to-day business of government.

Operates
Neighborhood parks, police/fire/911, sewers, libraries, buses

Who's in Charge
Mayor, city council

PARTY ON!

Political parties are a key feature of every democracy. These organizations put forth candidates for election. The parties frame debates and simplify choices for voters. All kinds of parties operate in the United States. In most elections, though, Americans get just two main choices—Democrat or Republican. The focus and ideas of each party have changed greatly over time. See how they stack up in recent years.

Outlook
Conservative
Laws should follow proven values from the past.

Presidential elections won from 1900–2012

 Hot Topics

End government health care
Ban abortion
Protect right to own guns

BIG IDEAS

Lower taxes
Less government spending
Keep business free from government
Military strength

Elephant

Republicans
a.k.a. Grand Old Party, GOP
Founded 1854

Famous Republican Presidents

Abraham Lincoln

Teddy Roosevelt

Ronald Reagan

RED, BLUE, AND PURPLE

Blue states tend to vote Democratic. Red states are more Republican, and purple states are "swing states." They could go either way.

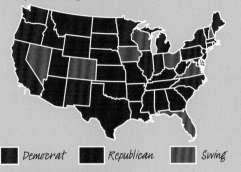

| ■ Democrat | ■ Republican | ■ Swing |

PARTY BREAKDOWN

People in cities tend to go Democrat, while country and suburban folks lean Republican. The parties also look different when you look at race and gender.

	White	Black	Hispanic	other
Democrat	61%	21%	10%	7%
Republican	87%	2%	5%	4%

	Men	Women
Democrat	43%	57%
Republican	52%	48%

Hot Topics

Gay marriage
Abortion rights
Clean energy
Government health care

Presidential elections won from 1900–2012

Outlook
Liberal
Laws should evolve to help fix economic and social problems.

BIG IDEAS

Expand civil rights

Protect the environment

Expand services for those in need, including school programs

Donkey

Democrats
Founded 1828

Famous Democratic Presidents

Franklin D. Roosevelt | John F. Kennedy | Bill Clinton

HOW TO BECOME PRESIDENT

Want to run for president? Start by raising money and drumming up support. Next, you'll need to beat out other candidates from your party. Then it's a battle between you and the other party's pick. The whole process takes about two years and almost $1 billion. Begin at GO.

Your first step is to beat out other candidates from your own party in state primaries.

PRIMARY SEASON

FUN FACT

Fund-raising is huge for candidates. President Barack Obama spent $985.7 million on his campaign in 2011 and 2012.

Polls suggest you have a chance at becoming president.

You spend 36 hours planning your big message. It's still fuzzy. Go back a space.

EARLY PLANNING

The steak at your fund-raising dinner tastes like rubber. Lose a turn.

GO!

THE BIG ANNOUNCEMENT

You announce your run for the presidency.

On Super Tuesday, as many as two dozen states hold primaries. You're losing big time. Go back to GO.

DOWN TO TWO

All other candidates from your party dropped out. Now it's you and the other party's candidate. Jump ahead 6 spaces.

As it turns out, your choice for vice president cheated on his taxes. Go back five spaces.

Your party's political convention begins. You officially become your party's candidate at this four-day media event.

You dominate during a live debate. Go ahead three spaces.

THE FINAL STRETCH

FUN FACT

Presidential campaigns have as many as 500 paid workers. Volunteers number in the hundreds of thousands.

CONGRATULATIONS!
You've been elected the next president!

Polls show you're ahead. Now you have to make sure people actually go and vote. You organize a "get out the vote" drive.

HAVE A VOICE, MAKE A CHOICE!

It's time to vote! Who goes to the polls? What do they do? Let's take a closer look at this all-important process.

BEHIND THE CURTAIN

In 2012, voters marked their choices three main ways.

Optical Scan
How-To
Fill in ovals on a paper ballot. Feed the ballots into a machine that counts them.
Share of all ballots: 56%

Electronic Voting Machines
How-To
Press buttons, turn dials, or touch a screen.
Share of all ballots: 39%

Paper Ballots
How-To
Mark an X next to your choice. People tally results.
Share of all ballots: 4%

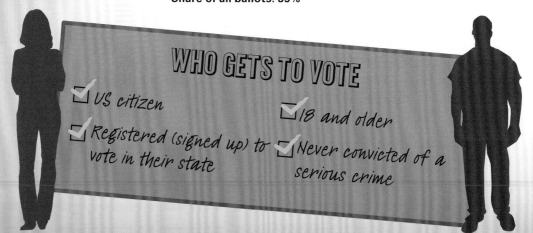

WHO GETS TO VOTE

- ☑ US citizen
- ☑ Registered (signed up) to vote in their state
- ☑ 18 and older
- ☑ Never convicted of a serious crime

VOTER TURNOUT

STATE
Minnesota had the highest rate of voter turnout. Hawaii came in last.

76%

44%

In 2012, just **61.8 percent** of adult citizens voted in the US presidential election. Some groups had better turnout than others.

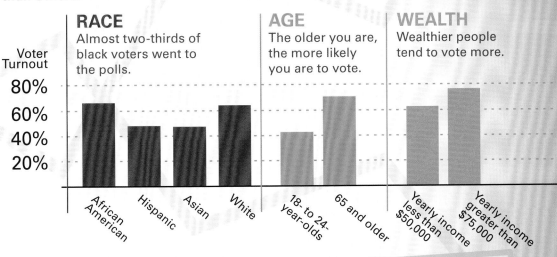

Voter Turnout

80%
60%
40%
20%

RACE
Almost two-thirds of black voters went to the polls.

African American

Hispanic

Asian

White

AGE
The older you are, the more likely you are to vote.

18- to 24-year-olds

65 and older

WEALTH
Wealthier people tend to vote more.

Yearly income less than $50,000

Yearly income greater than $75,000

WHY DIDN'T YOU VOTE?
Top reasons given by nonvoters:

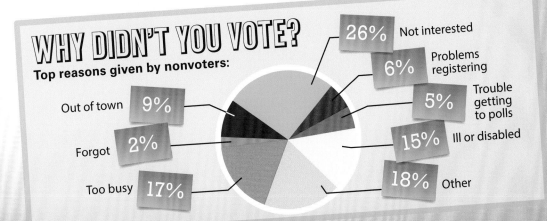

26% Not interested

6% Problems registering

5% Trouble getting to polls

15% Ill or disabled

18% Other

9% Out of town

2% Forgot

17% Too busy

LET'S TALK TAXES

That candy bar you want is 99 cents. But the cashier's asking for $1.04. What's the deal? That extra five cents is tax—money that goes to run the government. Paying taxes is the law. Federal, state, and local governments all offer ways to pay.

FEDERAL TAXES

INCOME TAX
Most people are charged taxes on the money they earn. Workers have taxes taken straight from their paychecks. A middle-class worker can expect to cough up about 16 percent of his or her salary.

SOCIAL SECURITY TAX
Another 6.2 percent goes to pay for Social Security. This federal program pays money to retired or disabled workers.

MEDICARE TAX
Another 1.5 to 2.4 percent of that paycheck goes to Medicare, a government health-care program.

STATE TAXES

EXCISE TAX
Most states charge extra taxes on gas, cigarettes, and alcohol.

SALES TAX
Most states tax the stuff you buy in stores. Groceries and medicine usually don't count.

INCOME TAX
All but nine states collect income taxes on paychecks. On average, middle-class workers pay about 5 percent of their paycheck. That's on top of what they've paid to the feds.

LOCAL TAXES

INCOME TAX
Some local governments charge income taxes. These rates typically run about 1 or 2 percent.

SALES TAX
Many cities and towns charge a sales tax—on top of the state one.

PROPERTY TAX
People pay taxes on their homes. A typical rate is 1 percent of a house's value.

MONEY WELL SPENT?

Every year, the federal government collects about $2.5 trillion (that's $2,500,000,000,000!) in taxes. Where does it go?

19% Military

22% Social Security

21% Health-care programs

12% Services for people in need

7% Benefits to veterans and retired federal workers

6% Interest payments on borrowed money

3% Transportation

2% Education

2% Scientific and medical research

1% Aid to other countries

5% Other

HARD AT WORK

More than four million people work for the federal government. Some 1.5 million are in the military. The rest make up about 2 percent of the US workforce. They are scientists, librarians, lawyers, bodyguards, and others. Take a look at some of the places they support through their work.

Postal Service
592,740

Smithsonian Institution
5,005

EPA
18,055

NASA
18,134

Social Security
65,114

Independent Agencies

Peace Corps
1,081

US Supreme Court
● **500**

US Courts
33,271

Judicial Branch

US House of Representatives
10,088

US Senate
7,030

Legislative Branch

Government Printing Office
2,378

● US Botanic Garden
66

KEY

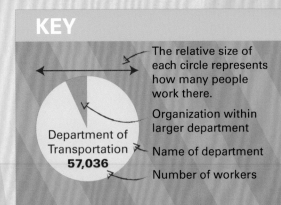

The relative size of each circle represents how many people work there.

Organization within larger department

Department of Transportation
57,036

Name of department

Number of workers

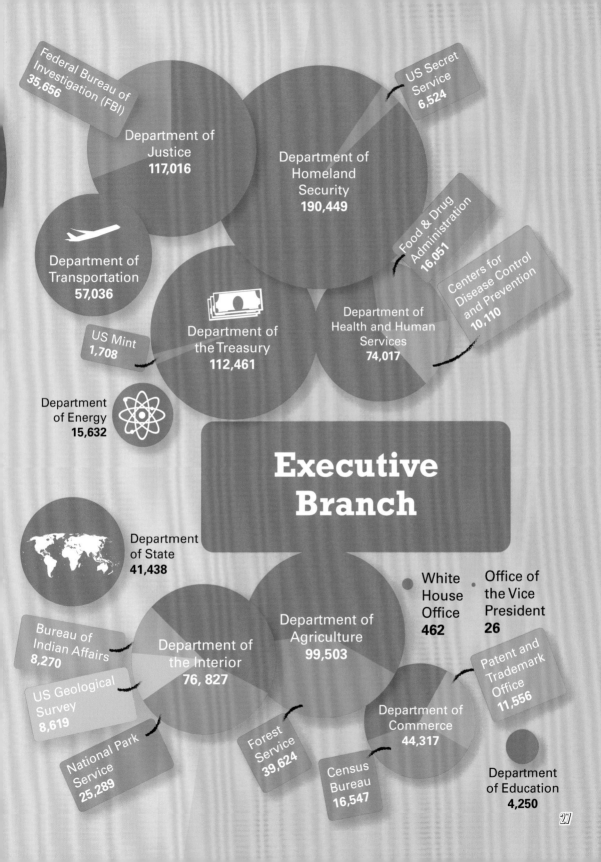

Federal Bureau of Investigation (FBI)
35,656

Department of Justice
117,016

US Secret Service
6,524

Department of Homeland Security
190,449

Food & Drug Administration
16,051

Centers for Disease Control and Prevention
10,110

Department of Transportation
57,036

US Mint
1,708

Department of the Treasury
112,461

Department of Health and Human Services
74,017

Department of Energy
15,632

Executive Branch

Department of State
41,438

Bureau of Indian Affairs
8,270

Department of the Interior
76, 827

Department of Agriculture
99,503

White House Office
462

Office of the Vice President
26

US Geological Survey
8,619

Patent and Trademark Office
11,556

National Park Service
25,289

Forest Service
39,624

Department of Commerce
44,317

Census Bureau
16,547

Department of Education
4,250

A CENTURY OF CHANGE

How much can a government change in 100 years? Take a look!

CABINET
The president has ten top advisers, including the postmaster general.

HOUSE OF REPRESENTATIVES
In 1911, the law caps the number of representatives at 435—about 1 for every 200,000 people.

SENATE
Starting in 1913, senators are elected directly by the people, instead of state legislatures.

SUPREME COURT
No cameras are allowed in the court.

WOMEN
Women are banned from voting. This would change in 1920.

1910s

PRESIDENT
Woodrow Wilson supports segregation. Some blacks in government jobs must use separate offices and bathrooms.

Woodrow Wilson

Presidential Inaugurations Then and Now

Presidents have been taking the oath of office in front of the US Capitol for more than 100 years! The background image on the left is a photo of President Woodrow Wilson's inaugural event. Wilson was president from 1913 to 1921. On the right is a photo from President Barack Obama's inaugural event. Obama was sworn into office in 2009.

2010s

CABINET
15 top advisers include secretaries of energy, education, and transportation.

HOUSE OF REPRESENTATIVES
Each member represents about 700,000 people.

SENATE
A senator spends an average of $9 million per election. Reformers seek to limit campaign costs.

SUPREME COURT
Cameras, including TV cameras, are still not allowed inside the stately chambers.

WOMEN
The Senate has 20 female members— the most ever.

PRESIDENT
Barack Obama is the first African American president.

Barack Obama

Glossary

AMENDMENT: a change to a law or document. *Amendment* often refers to one of the twenty-seven amendments to the US Constitution.

BALLOT: a form that people use to vote. Ballots allow voters to mark their choices in secret.

CABINET: a group of advisers to the president. Each cabinet member has his or her own special area of knowledge, such as education or defense.

CAMPAIGN: a series of events that is carefully planned to bring about a goal, such as winning an election

CANDIDATE: someone who is running for political office

CHECKS AND BALANCES: a system in which the different parts of a government can control or influence the other parts. Checks and balances limit the power of government.

CONSTITUTION: a document that lays out how a government will be organized. A constitution also expresses a nation's basic beliefs and goals.

FEDERALISM: a way of organizing a government where power is shared between a central government and smaller units, such as states. In the United States, the central government is boss, but states have their own areas of authority.

JUSTICE: a judge, especially one of the nine members of the US Supreme Court

PARLIAMENT: a body of elected representatives that make laws. Parliaments choose one of their members to head the government.

POLL: information gathered by asking people questions about their opinions; also, the place where people go to vote

PRIMARY: an election within a party to choose that party's candidate for office. Primaries happen several months before the general election.

REPRESENTATIVE: a government official elected by voters from a specific region. Representatives make laws on behalf of citizens.

SUFFRAGE: the right to vote. Suffrage for all adult citizens is a key feature of democracy.

VETO: to turn down a plan so that it cannot go forward. The president can veto a bill from Congress.

Further Information

Friedman, Mark. *The Democratic Process.* New York: Scholastic, 2012.
Get a close-up look at how our democracy works.

IRS: Understanding Taxes
http://apps.irs.gov/app
/understandingTaxes/student
/index.jsp
This government site for kids explains the "how and whys" of taxes.

Kids in the House
http://kids.clerk.house.gov
/middle-school
This is the official kids' site of the US House of Representatives, a go-to choice for basics and fun facts.

Landau, Elaine. *The President, Vice President, and Cabinet.* Minneapolis: Lerner Publications, 2012. Find out who staffs the executive branch and what they do.

Official Constitution of the United States
http://www.archives.gov/exhibits
/charters/constitution.html
Click around to discover specific parts of this historic document. Or just enjoy the fun facts and extra articles.

PBS Kids: The Democracy Project
http://pbskids.org/democracy
/my-government
Online games let you pretend to be president, vote on current issues, and more.

Ransom, Candice. *Who Wrote the US Constitution? And Other Questions about the Constitutional Convention of 1787.* Minneapolis: Lerner Publications, 2011. Learn the dramatic story of how the Constitution came to be.

Streetlaw: Landmark Cases of the Supreme Court
http://www.streetlaw.org/en
/landmark/home
Learn key info on the 17 most important Supreme Court cases of all time.

The White House: The Presidents
http://www.whitehouse.gov
/about/presidents
Enjoy a slide show, and while you're there, read the life stories of our nation's presidents.

LERNER
SOURCE
Expand learning beyond the printed book. Download free, complementary educational resources for this book from our website, www.lerneresource.com.

Index

PHOTO ACKNOWLEDGMENTS
The photos in this book are used with the permission of: National Archives
(1667751), pp. 12, 13 top, 13 middle; National Archives (1408042), p. 13
bottom; Library of Congress, pp. 18 left (LC-USZ62-13016), middle (LC-DIG-
ppmsca-35950), 19 left (LC-USZ62-117121), middle (LC-USZ62-117124), 28
inset (LC-USZ62-13028); United States Department of Defense, pp. 18 right,
19 right; Architect of the Capitol, p. 28 (background); Senior Master Sgt.
Thomas Meneguin/US Air Force/United States Department of Defense, p. 29
background; The White House, p. 29 inset.